Secrets of Relationships

A compilation of Talks, given by

GURUDEV SRI SRI RAVI SHANKAR

SECRETS OF RELATIONSHIPS

Talks by Gurudev Sri Sri Ravi Shankar

1st Edition 2008

Published by:

THE ART OF LIVING

Sri Sri Publications Trust
The Art of Living International Centre,
21st KM, Kanakapura Road, Udayapura, Bangalore – 560082.
Email: info@srisripublications.com
Website: www.sattvastore.com
Toll Free: 1800-258-8888

ISBN: 9789380114828

Layout by: Sri Sri Publications Trust

Printed in India by: Jwalamukhi Mudranalaya Pvt. Ltd., Bangalore
Ph: +91-80-26601064, 26617243

CONTENTS

PREFACE

One of the world's most inspirational and dynamic leaders, Gurudev Sri Sri Ravi Shankar, is also one of the most original thinkers of our times. Emphasising practical wisdom, He has transformed millions of lives all over the globe. His talks are a unique blend of knowledge and guidance, delivered with simplicity and humour - a powerful, unbeatable combination that touches lives and hearts, wherever heard.

It is with great joy that we offer this stunningly insightful collection of profound, yet simple to comprehend talks, given by Gurudev Sri Sri Ravi Shankar, over a period of time, unravelling the secrets of relationships.

FINDING REAL COMMUNICATION

Head-to-head communication is through thoughts and words, while heart-to-heart communication is through feelings. People, throughout the ages, have felt that they cannot communicate their feelings. If we could communicate all our feelings through words, then we would be living very shallow lives. Life is rich because feelings cannot be captured in words! So we use all these gestures – we hug, so that hearts come closer, we give flowers, so that feelings are conveyed… We put all our efforts into expressing our feelings… and still, feelings remain unexpressed.

Soul-to-soul communication is silence. When we transcend the feeling level, we become still. Stillness is at the peak of any experience – that's why the saying, "Be still… and know your God".

When our eyes are open, we are lost in activity, and when our eyes are closed, we fall asleep. So we miss the point – the point is in-between closing our eyes, and not falling asleep.

Meditation means seeing God within you, and love is seeing God in the person next to you. The two complement each other. The more you serve, the deeper you are able to go within.

We find two types of people in the world – those, who are just focused on themselves; on improving themselves, and those, who are lost in serving. Those, who are lost in serving, get tired, frustrated, angry… and then their service also suffers.

Some boy-scouts were at a Sunday service, when the Father (priest) said, "You should serve."

They asked, "What is this service?"

He said, "Suppose, an old woman wants to cross a road, go and help her cross the road."

So the boys went and looked for a whole week, but there was no old woman, trying to cross a street. Finally, four of them found a woman walking on a footpath. One of the boys went and asked her, "Madam, would you like to cross the road?"

She turned and said, "No."

He was disappointed. So another boy went and asked her again, thinking, perhaps, that the first boy hadn't asked properly. He asked, "Would you like to cross the road?"

The woman was now a little bit confused. She wondered why she was being asked this. So she said, it was all right for him to take her across the road.

Once they'd reached the other side, a third boy came and asked her, "Would you like to cross the road?"

Now it really bothered her.

When the fourth one approached her, she almost screamed, and ran away!

We think this is service! Service is *not* just *doing* something. It is that consciousness within you, where you are readily available to do something. Often people first say, "No!" and then, they think of saying, "Yes!"

You know, if someone asks you, "Would you like to give me a ride?" you first say, "No!"... and then, "Okay." You may give the person a ride, but when you have already said "No" in the first place, the consciousness has already twisted somewhere. Service is seeing God in the next person, and when we serve, we are able to go deep within... The deeper you go, the more you are able to serve. They complement each other. Hmmm…

Now tell me, what topic, would you like me to speak on?

[Audience says: Abundance. Forgiveness. Seeing God in everyday activity. Appreciation. Love. Courage. Rivalry. Trust…]

Okay… Does it really matter, what topic we speak about? Are you all here, one hundred percent? If you're hungry, you may be going to a restaurant, in your mind! You're sitting in this church, but thinking about lasagne and pizza! Hmmm?

Abundance! How does one feel abundant? Right?

Know, you belong to God, and all that you need, will be given to you at the moment you need.

What is the sign of success? Everyone wants to be successful, but what is the sign of success? Worries, tension, diabetes, ulcers, blood pressure, fear and anxiety? No! A smile! A smile that cannot be stolen by anybody!

So, suppose you're in business, and you make one million dollars in profit. Do you know what a successful man would do? What will he do? Keep the one million dollars with him? No! He will borrow nine million more from the bank! That's a sign of success, right? Getting into greater debt! Now, who is richer – one who has a thousand dollar debt, or one who has a one million dollar debt?!

See, America is the most successful country in the whole world today… and it is America that is in the greatest debt too. Do you see that? So abundance is not just amassing money, or keeping a big bank balance; abundance is a state of consciousness – when you *feel* you have plenty. Remember the saying from the Bible: "Those, who have, more will be given to them. Those, who do not have, whatever little they have, will also be taken away from them." Feel the abundance within you… and you can only feel this, when you feel connected to the Divine. There is *no* other way. When you feel connected to the innermost God within you, then nobody can take your smile away from you; no one can ever induce any fear into you, and then, you will have compassion, for the world, flowing out of you.

Forgiveness can never be complete, you know. We struggle, trying to forgive someone else. Do you know why? When you say, "I forgive," you think that the person, you are saying it to, is a culprit, and when you think someone is a culprit, and then try to forgive him (or her), however you do it, a little bit of it still remains. It's not complete. But, when you see the grand picture – the big picture – you will see that the culprit is also a victim – a victim of his (or her) own mind, ignorance, unawareness, or unconsciousness. Isn't it? Don't you think so? So compassion arises from within you, when you cannot forgive someone else.

There is a story about Buddha. A gentleman found out that all his sons, daughters, daughters-in-law – everybody in his family – were going to Buddha's meditation sessions. He found out that they were all sitting and meditating, and this was something he didn't like – something he couldn't tolerate. His children wouldn't listen to him, and so this well-respected businessman went to Buddha. There was an assembly of 10,000 people sitting in front of Buddha. The man went up to Buddha and spat on his face. Buddha never said a word. He just smiled back… There was such compassion radiating out from Buddha's face, from his whole being, that this man just could not stand it… and he ran away from that place. He could not sleep the whole night. This was the first time that someone had not reacted to him. And something happened – the Divine took over him. The next morning, he was a transformed person, and he went and fell at Buddha's feet, asking for forgiveness.

Buddha said, "I cannot forgive you. The person, whom you spat on, is here no more now, and there is no chance that I will ever meet him again. Also, you are not the same person now. The person, who spat on me yesterday, is not the same one, who is bowing down today."

There is no way to forgive. Compassion is a step higher. However, when people cannot understand compassion, then they have to be spoken to in terms of forgiveness. See, knowledge is given to the place – to the people, who need it at that time. Of course, it contains the eternal Truth – the Truth that is beyond time – but, the outer covering, the outer expression, will be according to the time, the people, the place.

Buddha was addressing a refined society – people of a high intellectual calibre. At that time, the people were all highly intellectual. It was a stress-free society already.

However, when Jesus had to talk, he had to talk to people, who were in great suffering. He had to talk to laymen, people, who were not literate – illiterates. Often Jesus has said that he would say something several times, but the people would not understand, and so he had to repeat it, modify it, or say it in another way. He had to use two-three parables. The time was different. When Jesus gave his teachings, the people were in the darkest period of time, of history... Still, the essence is the same – the essence, whether you call it compassion, or you call it forgiveness, it is the same. Hmmm?

Love! Love is responsible for all our negative emotions! If there were no love on this planet, then there wouldn't have been any problem at all – nobody would ever be jealous; nobody would ever be greedy; no one would ever get angry at anything. Anger, greed, jealousy – all the negative emotions, we've experienced, are all fruits of love. Isn't this true?

How can you be jealous without loving?! Impossible! You love perfection, and so you're angry at imperfection – you cannot stand imperfection.

But, no one ever wants these "fruits". They want love in its purity, in its perfection... and it is the knowledge of one's self, alone, that can do this. As Reverend Michael* said earlier, just wake up and see – Everything is changing! The whole world around you is changing. When we don't understand that everything is changing, then we get stuck; we feel the whole world is a load on our heads – but, just the awareness that everything is changing, makes you feel lighter.

The illusion in the mind that "the world is going to give me joy," keeps one hooked to the "outside" – but, if you have absorbed moments of joy, you always go within.

Suppose you smell something very beautiful – a very good fragrance – then, automatically, your eyes shut. Have you noticed this? If you taste something great, you close your eyes: "Ahh! Great! Lasagne – It's delicious! Ice-cream! It's delicious!" You don't

**A speaker, who preceded Gurudev at this talk*

know, who made it, or how one makes it, but you enjoy it anyway… and you close your eyes – people, who enjoy it, enjoy it, and in the moment of that enjoyment, one closes one's eyes. It is the same with the sense of touch, the sense of smell; even with music – when you listen to great music, your eyes shut automatically… and you go deep inside, isn't it? So the source of joy is within us, but we hook it to an object outside. People in California think that going to Vancouver is great because of the snowy mountains there, and people in Vancouver – you know, those who are high up in Whistler – they think, they dream, of coming to California, to L.A.! We think joy is somewhere else. As long as we are not used to a place, we think joy is there, but, once we get used to it, joy is no longer there anymore. For people living in the countryside, Hollywood is their dream… and for people in Hollywood – well, they would like to go to the countryside!

We experience joy in-between the objects. When we change from one thing to another, we seem to experience joy, but we associate that joy, which comes from the gap, with the next object, and so there is a rat-race, which goes on with respect to that object. God is *not* an object. God is not an object of sight, sound, smell, taste or touch. God is the innermost experience of the heart. Only the heart can know God – not the mind, not the intellect, not reading volumes of books, nor listening to talks – just simple innocence from deep within… Hmmm...

Trust… To understand trust, you must know what doubt is. Without knowing doubt, you cannot grow in trust – It's impossible!

If you don't have trust – never mind! Do you have doubt? Have you looked at the doubt that you have? Have you observed the doubt, you have? It's very interesting… You always doubt something that is positive! If someone tells you, "I love you very much!" –you ask him (or her), "Really?" If someone tells you, "I hate you!" – you never ask, "Really?!" You doubt your capabilities – you never doubt your incapabilities. You are sure of what you cannot do, but you doubt what you can do! Isn't it?

You doubt the honesty of someone. You doubt love and happiness. When you are happy, you doubt – "I'm not sure… Is this what I want?" But, when you are depressed, you never doubt – "Am I really depressed?" When you are happy, you're not sure; you're never sure that you are happy – but depression never brings a question of doubt! So our doubt is always about something that is good, something that is positive! So if you doubt God, I think it's great! Don't struggle! If you're doubting God, that means you trust God. We doubt in the existence of God, we doubt in the people around us… and then, we doubt ourselves. Just knowing this, you transcend doubt, and you get onto that platform of trust, which is unshakeable. Nothing whatsoever can take it out of you. Then, you feel, everyone belongs to you. All bodies are just like shells in the ocean. We are in an ocean of consciousness, an ocean of life… and every human body, or animal body (or whatever it is) is just like a shell floating in the ocean… and expressing divinity… holding that water…

❄❄❄

INTERPERSONAL RELATIONSHIPS

What should we discuss today? Any topic?

[Audience says: Interpersonal relationships!]

It is very important to know about interpersonal relationships – What keeps them going… and what really disturbs them. So let us look into this. Is that okay with all of you?

[Audience says: Yes!]

Interpersonal relationships get disturbed, when disagreement begins. As long as there is agreement, they don't get disturbed at all. So what disturbs a relationship?

Disagreement.

Now, take a look at yourself... Have you always agreed with yourself? Huh?

[Audience says: No]

You have *not* agreed. You had an idea yesterday... and today, you have a different idea! Five years back, you had different ideas, and they did not necessarily agree with the ideas, you have today. So, when you can have a disagreement with yourself, why not with someone else, next to you?! The person, with whom you have a disagreement, is just an old photocopy of your own self; a copy of your old self – or maybe even a new copy! What you disagree with today, you may agree on, three years from now. So, you need to take a look at your own thought patterns and your emotional patterns.

As you know, there is a rhythm in nature. Isn't it? At particular times, seasons come, and then nature responds. Similarly, you know, we have several rhythms in our system. There is a rhythm in the body; there is a bio-rhythm – e.g. hunger and all those other things. There is a rhythm in the thought patterns. If you observe your patterns – your thought patterns – you will find, there is a rhythm there. Similarly, there is a rhythm in the emotions and our breath. And finally, there is a rhythm in the consciousness – the soul – that we are. We need to find harmony between all these rhythms within us, and *that* is called spirituality.

Spirituality is not just fantasizing. It is observing your own existence.

What is here right now?

Our body is here right now – but have we known our body, thoroughly? You can know another's body, but have you experienced your *own* body?

Experiencing your own body, your breath, your mind, your emotions, and the source of your life, *is* meditation. Did you get it? Am I clear? Is it clear?

What is meditation?

Meditation is experiencing the life-force, or being conscious of the life-force... and it's not done with effort. It is something that is done effortlessly. I'd say that the mind and the body function on completely opposite laws. (You might have heard of this before...)

In the realm of the mind, effortlessness is the key. You cannot remember something, if you put effort into it – but the moment you relax, the memory comes back! Creativity, intelligence and memory – all these faculties within us happen effortlessly. However, you can only build muscles, when you put in effort! You go to a gym... and when there is no pain, there is no gain! Or these days, it's the reverse – when there is no pain, there is no loss! If you have to lose your tummy, you have to work out! So, no pain – no loss!

Are you all with me, as I am speaking? Are you listening to me?

[Audience says: Yes!]

How are you listening?

The sounds come, and fall on your eardrums, but if the mind is elsewhere, can you hear me?

[Audience says: No!]

You are listening, through that faculty in you, that's called the "mind".

Are you looking at me? If your mind is elsewhere, you can't see! You are seeing, smelling and hearing. The perceptual ability of consciousness – we call, the mind. Do you agree with me?

As I am speaking, you are agreeing… or disagreeing.

Are you agreeing? Are you saying, "Yes"? Are you aware, you are saying, "Yes"? Or, are you saying, "No"? Are you aware you are saying, "No"?

The intellect is something, by which, we say, "Yes!" or "No!"

Yes?

No?

[Laughter!]

The same consciousness functions as *mann* (mind), *buddhi* (intellect), *chitta* (memory) and *ahankaara* (ego). These four different *antahkaran chadushtaya*, are what our ancient people called, the four different faculties.

So similarly, if you observe the memory, you will see that our memory clings onto something negative.

You'll forget all the ten compliments, you received, but the one insult, you got, sticks in the mind! This tendency of the mind needs to be reversed... and the process of reversing this tendency of the mind, from clinging to the negative, to moving to something positive, is called "*yoga*". The technology or process is called *yoga*. Isn't it so essential? What does it do?

Yoga makes you like a baby again! It not only revives your nature, but it also makes your heart young, and keeps your mind, young and bright. *Yoga* improves perception, observation and expression.

So, coming back to interpersonal relationships... You have to have a relationship with *yourself*. What is your relationship with yourself?

Your relationship with yourself, is what is called integrity, and if you have no relationship with yourself, that is called a lack of integrity. Yes? Do you agree?

Being informal is another thing that will keep your interpersonal relationships strong. Informality is the giving of space for mistakes to happen. In any relationship, in any situation, you can't expect perfection – there will be flaws. However, if your mind is vast, big and accommodative of all situations, then your relationship does not get disturbed at all; otherwise, you become an emotional yo-yo – unstable. Do you see what I am saying? Today, one of the biggest problems with the world is emotional instability.

So, when we create an informal outlook, and a cordial environment around us, then, that will grease the friction… and you will be the master of your environment and not feel helpless about what is happening around you.

❄❄❄

ADOLESCENTS AND THE ELDERLY

PART I: THE TEENAGE YEARS…

You know, the "teens" are the most confusing age! You are no longer a kid, who can be pacified with toys or sweets, but neither are you emotionally mature enough. A new world has just opened up in front of you… and it's such a difficult time. On one hand, there are big highs; on the other hand, there are a lot of lows! There's also loneliness. A child doesn't feel lonely, but a teenager starts feeling lonely. Not only that, there are also so many hormonal changes happening in the body. So he (or she) is getting familiar with his (or her) own body, mind, emotions, urges and difficulties.

Suddenly, teenagers feel nobody understands them because what parents say from their standpoint –

good or bad – doesn't appeal to them. Long-term plans don't exist! They want immediate solutions, immediate gratification; everything should happen *now*! Teenagers feel that adults do not understand, but they don't feel connected with small kids either because they feel it's meaningless, it's useless – all the toys, all the simple games, which they have outgrown.

During these tough times of the teenage years, the kids need to have hope. They need to have an understanding about life. They need to know what they want to do and how to deal with what they want, right?

There is an old saying in Sanskrit: "When your son or daughter turns sixteen, behave with them like a friend. Don't be their teachers. Don't tell them what they should, or shouldn't be doing, but share with them their difficulties. Be a friend to them."

You know, a friend is one, who is on your level. A friend understands you, moves with you, with your emotions, with your difficulties. He stands in the same shoes. So if you behave as a friend to them and not as a parent, they open up to you. Usually teenagers open up much more to their friends, their pals, than to their parents! It's a common phenomenon. So also teachers! A teacher should also be a friend; behave as a friend, talk as a friend. Then the gap gets bridged. Once the gap is bridged, love flows – Communication happens. Once communication happens, the problem is solved! Most of the problem is a lack of communication.

Now emotions – what does one do with one's emotions? It's a big problem! Although we may have grown older – beyond the 'teen' age – sometimes, we have still not grown beyond the 'teen' age, mentally! You know, there is a particular cycle, in which our body grows. In the first seven years, the physical body grows – it grows from age fourteen to twenty-one years, even. So the body has a seven-year growth cycle – the fourteen-year growth and the twenty-one-year growth. In the first seven years, the intellect does not grow – just the body. Then up to fourteen years, the intellect grows. You cannot improve someone's IQ power after they have turned fifteen. This is the general thinking or understanding, that children under fourteen can learn many things very quickly.

So, you become physically mature, then intellectually mature, and then emotionally mature. The period from fourteen to twenty-one years is for emotional maturity. Many do not grow to that maturity at all! Lack of emotional maturity means you are always worrying about your emotions; feeling as though you are a victim of your own emotions, "Oh! I feel like this! What to do?"

What do you do? Who cares about your feelings?! Why do you worry so much about your feelings? You know, we feel as though we are victimized by our own emotions! "Oh! I feel so bad..." You feel so bad, so what?! You feel bad... and a little later, it turns, and you feel good! Your feelings keep changing. Sometimes you feel bad, but it doesn't stay for your whole life! It turns and then you feel good, and then that doesn't stay for the whole time. You feel good and then you feel bad again. Nobody can stay, feeling bad all the time or feeling good all the time. These good and bad feelings come like waves. You can't stop a wave that has already come, nor can you make a wave come just like that. Isn't it? Just as waves and clouds come and go, the emotions come and go. Different waves of emotion come and then they disappear! Making them into a big issue and complaining in our minds, "Oh! I feel good! Oh! I feel bad! Oh! I feel this way

Oh! I feel that way and nobody cares for me! Nobody does this and nobody does that…" all this emotional garbage that we put into our heads is useless! It is a sign of a lack of emotional maturity. You see what I'm saying? Emotional maturity, intellectual maturity and physical maturity, you need all three of these "maturities". Then you are a complete personality!

Are you sharp and focused? Are you interested in learning? This shows how you have matured intellectually. Then, do not let emotional immaturity cloud your intellect. This is what happens! Emotions that are not mature cloud the intellect. If your emotions are not mature enough, you're caught up in them all the time. Isn't it? What do you say? So, by the age of twenty-one, you are supposed to be so strong emotionally, physically and intellectually sharp. Then you get the power to vote. You're supposed to be an adult, you're supposed to be mature, but this seldom happens!

What is the big deal about your feelings? I tell you bundle them up and throw them in the ocean! Then you can be happy! Then you are in good spirits! Just examine why your spirit goes down…

Somebody said something stupid to you – and your spirit goes down. Now, why did they say that stupid thing?

They said that stupid thing because they had some garbage and they threw it out… and you were there, ready to catch it, saying, "Oh! I won't give this away!"

Why did somebody insult you?

They insulted you because they were hurt, they had garbage in them, and they wanted to throw it out. When they threw it out, you passionately grabbed it and kept it in your pocket! "So and so hurt me! They did this, they did that!"

Come one, wake up! Get up and walk! Don't let your smile be snatched away by anybody! In the world, not everything will happen perfectly, all the time! In every action, there can be imperfections. Even the best or greatest of actions with good intentions, will have some imperfections. Unfortunately, the tendency is to go and grab the imperfection and make yourself, your mood, imperfect; make your mind imperfect, make your soul reel in this nonsense. Isn't that so? So we need to get out of these cycles and be strong and courageous from within... and that, which gives you the strength, the courage and the smile, is called spirituality. Anything that helps you to become unconditionally happy and loving is called spirituality.

PART II: THE ELDERLY…

Old people are not any different from children! You should treat them like kids. Like children, they are adamant and repeat the same things! They talk about the same thing over and over again, without realizing they have already said it several times! When a pattern sets in them, you accept them as they are. They are the best practical example for you to demonstrate that you have followed the first principle of the Art of Living – "Accept people as they are". They come into your life and make you realize that. You cannot change old people overnight, or even in a period of time. You need to accept them. That is how they are, and it is all right to have their point of view.

See, there is some wisdom in what they are saying. Sometimes, you are unable to see wisdom in what an experienced, mature person says. They speak from their own experience, over the years. So in dealing with them, you need to know that they are experienced and that they have a different set of experiences, much different from yours. So we accept them as they are. Second, we don't get upset because they don't change! If you get upset, it only makes it worse. By your not accepting them, they are not going to change. So you accept them as they are because you are too small to change them, and you will find a miracle happening! The moment you accept them and give them a space of love and compassion, they slowly start changing. They do change! So you need to have a lot of patience. You will learn patience dealing with old people, with grannies, who have certain patterns!

Also, don't take their moods too seriously! Suppose they're upset, don't take it too seriously because if you take it too seriously, then you are not able to communicate with them. Don't try to convince them too much. Sometimes, they just want to pour out their heart to you. If they are grumbling, they are just grumbling. They're saying it, but they don't really mean it! If they say, "I'm so upset" – they may say it, but they will still go and have their food, watch television and do all their things – but when they see you, they say, "Oh, I'm so upset, I never ate food, I didn't do this, I didn't do that!" If you take all their complaints seriously, you become miserable and life becomes miserable for you. So what should you do? When they complain to you about how bad life is, how bad people are, how much worse the whole world is and how miserable they are, you should simply take it and all those words with a little margin. Know that it is just their pattern. They're saying it, fine. It's okay. If you don't do this and take all their words too seriously, you can't sleep! You will lose your night's sleep and you will get depressed as well. You won't be able to help them.

People, who are very aged or sick, just want to communicate with you and in the process of communication, what is it that they can share with you?

When people don't have enthusiasm in them, they will only share their grievances. If they are piled up with grievances, they will only talk about this to you, but that doesn't mean that they are so miserable. There is a corner in them that remains untouched by any amount of misery. I tell you this is a fact. Whether it is extreme joy or happiness or terrible misery, there is a part in every human being that remains untouched by that. We need to realize that we have such a part inside us.

It is the same with people, who appear to be very miserable. In reality, they are not that miserable, but they talk, talk, talk and talk! The same people will have a party and will laugh, but the tendency of the mind is like that. Especially, when you know that someone cares for you, you don't always go to him (or her) with a smile and with joy – You go to him (or her) with all your problems and complaints! This is the normal course of things. This is what happens in the world. Isn't that so?

Suppose you are at a big party. At that party, you will go find your very close friend and complain, "The party is good, but this should have been better and that should have been better. They should have put that thing there. This light is not good. That curtain is a little crooked and you know there is no salt in this food – did you taste the food?!" Among the twenty items, you took one item and said, "Oh, this doesn't taste as good! Oh! The party where I went on the 25th of last month, that was very good." These complaints, you only make to your close friend(s), and go blah, blah, blah... You will find them and you'll talk, but you won't talk to the host! Out of manners, you won't go and tell someone new! The same happens with elderly people!

When they find someone very close to them, their confidantes (in whom they can confide things) – especially grandchildren, sons or daughters – have come home, then they will complain: "You know, your aunt is like that, she did this, she never even sent a Christmas greeting to me. I sent her three cards and she never even replied with one card!" These are the things that go on in their minds! They'll say all those things. But, I tell you, don't imagine that they're stuck with those things! Sometimes in their minds, these complaints don't even come, other than when they are with you! They say all that and then forget the whole thing! This is what happens as age advances.

There is a nice story. A man earned a lot of money and then gave all his property to his son. When his son got everything, he built a small outhouse behind the main house for his parents and he told them, "Now you have to stay there." So the old couple stayed there, while their son and his family started living in the big bungalow. One day, while playing, the grandchild came into his grandfather's home, where everything was old and in a very poor, pathetic condition – old utensils, old chairs, all the unwanted goods. Things that could break at any time were kept in that house. So the grandchild came and told his grandpa, "Grandpa, be careful with your plate and your chair. Don't break them!" When he asked why, the child said, "Because tomorrow my father needs all this." The child's father heard this and was shocked. That little boy saying, "Grandpa don't break it because tomorrow when I grow older, I'm also going to send my father here. So better save this!"

One does not realize this fact. *You* are also going to be old one day, and are going to be like them.

You ask, "Dad, where did you keep your book?"

He says, "What did you say? Nobody's at the door."

You ask, "Dad, are you coming with me?"

He says, "What did you say? You want a cup of water? There's plenty of it there!"

You will also get into such a state one day.

They tell you, what you should not be doing in your life. Tomorrow, you had better watch that you don't start complaining like them, and better you start that today itself! If you find that the grannies in your home are complaining, and you don't like it, you better not do it today, and if you see them as being so generous, so calm, so serene, so loving, you better start being that way right now. So you can learn both ways. You can learn what you should be doing and what you should not be doing from elderly people. And I tell you, if you're on the path, in the knowledge, and if you keep doing your meditations and the *Sudarshan Kriya*, your aging reverses! That enthusiasm to learn will exist and your alertness, focus, attention – everything – increases in life. You will not become cynical and senile as you advance in age.

If you are only focused, all the time, on pleasure, on what you will get, on how you can exploit others, or how you can enjoy, then you will see that the ability to enjoy, for your senses, is limited. Your senses will get so tired, and before that, they'll make your brain and mind tired, and you'll be in a "mumbo-jumbo mess". We have to sort ourselves out and get out of this mess. Wake up! Wake up and see: "Who am I? What am I? What is this world? What do I want? What can I do in this world? What did I do this last year to the world? What can I do this year to the world?" This zeal and enthusiasm, you have to create within yourself! Elderly people remind you: "Look! Don't become like me or you will follow in my footsteps". These are the two messages you get from them – either "you follow in my footsteps" or "you'd better not become like me"!

If you see pictures of Mahatma Gandhi, when he was young, he looked like a "Most Wanted" person, who was wanted dead or alive in twenty-seven robbery cases! But, as he became older, his smile became bigger because he started serving, he started meditating. His beauty increased everyday as he became older, because his quest for Truth was so great. So that fire in us: "I want to know the Truth. My life is committed to Truth, to knowing the Truth. My life is committed to serving everybody in the world and to make a better world around me. My life is committed to making myself useful to everybody!" This one thought can bring so much fire in you.

❄❄❄

THE SECRETS OF RELATIONSHIPS

First comes attraction. You are attracted to someone… but, if you get, what you are attracted to, very easily, the charm goes away – it dies out very fast. However, if what you are attracted to, becomes just a little bit difficult to have, then you develop love for it. Have you experienced this? Have you observed this?

Now, you fall in love! Then what happens?

After a while, the soap opera begins!

It is because you love someone, that you give yourself… and then you start making demands on that relationship. Now, when you start demanding, love diminishes. All the thrill, joy – everything – seems to be fading away. So then you say, "Oh! I have made a mistake!" Now there's struggle and pain to get out of it… and after you've got out of it, you get into another relationship – one more relationship – and the same story repeats itself!

What is it that you want to know about relationships? It is really to see, how they can be long-lasting. Isn't it? What is the secret about relationships, you want to know? You want to know, how they can be made long-lasting, not how they can be cut off – that, of course, is no secret!! Everybody knows about that – just push a button, or a few more buttons, very often! That's it! The relationship will be finished!

Three things are essential in any relationship – right perception, right observation and right expression. Often, people say that nobody understands them. Instead of saying, "No one understands me…" you can say that you have not expressed yourself properly. If you speak Russian to a Spaniard, he (or she) will definitely not understand! To express yourself properly, you need proper or right perception. Right perception can happen, when you see yourself, in the shoes of the other person – when you stand in his (or her) shoes and look at the situation.

One requires right perception and right observation. So, okay, you have perceived right, but how do you react? How do you feel inside? What motivates you? What things are coming up from within you?

Observing your own mind is essential – This is the second important aspect. This observation within you – the observation of sensations, the observation of tendencies, the observation of the patterns we have – is also essential. Perception of the other, and observation of one's self… and then comes – right expression, or expressing one's self in the right manner.

One's whole life is a lesson on just these three things – perception, observation and expression. Every mistake, you make, is not really a mistake – it's a learning process of the three vital aspects of life. What do you say? Isn't this so?

Perception needs to be expanded. Don't just see someone's "outside". If someone is grumpy, or a little finicky, we hold him (or her) responsible for his (or her) behaviour –but, if we see from a wide-angle lens, the many aspects will come together: "Okay, that person is finicky, or fussy, or stressed out, for some reason… and that is reflecting in the relationship". So, widening our lens of perception, and not just looking at someone and accusing them, for what they are doing (or what they did), but rather accommodating them, and seeing things from a larger picture (perspective), will help in relationships. This is the first secret.

The second thing is to give… This, of course, you all know! Relationships mean giving… and at the same time, make the others give also! Suppose, you are doing all the service, all the help, and you don't give the other person, something to do in return, you are taking their self-worth away from them. Sometimes people say, "Oh! See! I did so much, but that person still doesn't love me. Why??"

This is because they feel uncomfortable. Love is, when there is an exchange… and that can happen, when you give them an opportunity to *also* do something for you. This needs a little skill. You know, we have to be skilful in making the other also contribute, without us demanding. The only way we know to get someone to do something for us is by demand! Then, if your partner doesn't do something for you, love cannot last either because you will take on a self-pitying role saying, "See, I do everything! I've been used." You say, "I'm being used." So, you also make use of them, if your love needs to grow! This thing – "I'm being used" – should be taken out of our consciousness. You should know that you are being useful – that's why you're used! If you're useless, how can somebody use you?! Most relationships end up this way because we don't have the skill to make the other person contribute. Don't you think so? Isn't it so?

You know, in India, in the ancient times, they called "skilful taking", *dakshina*. In ancient times, children were taken to these schools, where they would study with the Master (the teacher) for seven-eight years, even twelve years. At the end of the twelfth year, they had to give something back in return – the thanks to the teacher, the fee, and this fee that they would give, was called *dakshina* – that, which is given with great skill. You know, it's very interesting how they would do that. They had a common classroom for everybody. So whether the students were princes, or paupers, they had to all study in one class. Now, suppose, a rich boy and a poor boy, were both studying in the same class, then the Master would ask the pauper (the very poor child) to bring money, and the child of the prince, to do some menial job.

Now, the boy, who was from the poor family, had to bring ten gold coins. What would he do? He had no means. If the same had been told to the prince, it would have been very easy to get – that student could bring a hundred gold coins, it was so easy for him. But this poor boy would go around, he would write poems, he would make art, he would make drawings, he would come up with some drama, or scriptures, or whatever. He would use all his creativity to get that money and come. So even the process of giving would expand his ability... and he would gain so much confidence: "Yes! I have been asked to bring ten gold coins. If I didn't have the ability, the Master wouldn't have told me to do so. He told me I can do it, so I'll be able to do it!" He would move with that confidence, he would go here and there, and he would get it. In this process of gaining these ten gold coins, his abilities, his skills, would all come out.

In the same way, the prince would be asked to go and do some menial job, like clean the streets. He would know and understand how a servant feels, and so he becomes sensitive. His sensitivity towards people would grow, though he would live in a palace. That's why this sort of exchange was called *dakshina*.

In a relationship, this is essential. You have to see that the other also contributes in your life, so that they don't feel completely like a worm – worthless

– but that they also feel their self-worth. For love to blossom, self-worth is essential. This is the second important point… or secret.

The third aspect of a relationship is to give the other space. When you love someone, you're right "on his (or her) neck"! You don't give them any breathing space… and they suffocate – and suffocation destroys love. You should give them space… and you take your space. Respect each other's space. Take some time off.

The ancient people knew this. You know, they would say that for one month in a year, a husband and wife could not cross the same door. So they would send the wives to their mothers' homes… and that would be the month that the postal department had the maximum business because that one month creates so much longing!! So they would write poems to each other – all the creativity in them would come out.

Love letters would flow from one city to another city.

For love to blossom, there needs to be longing… and longing needs a little space. Though it is a little painful, longing is inevitable. If there is no longing, if you destroy longing, if you don't allow longing to come into your relationship, then love does not grow. The charm is lost. So, give them some space… and take some space, yourself.

The fourth aspect in a relationship is that a relationship should be treated as the dessert, not as the main course! If your life is aimed at some goal, if there is some goal in your life, some aim in your life, then you move in that direction… and the relationship will move along. If all your focus is just on the relationship, I tell you, *that* is when it will not work… and it doesn't work! You can't have dessert for your main course. You cannot eat it like that. See, if you have a goal in your life, and if both of you have the same goal, you will move along in that direction. Then, that relationship lasts long. What do you say? Of course, I'm not an authority on this subject!

Whatever I speak, is from observation, you know, from my perception of what is happening in the world. This has been the story from ages!

You have a particular aim – to do something in life, to achieve something in life. You have a goal to do some service – you know, living your life for everyone's sake. You know how much money you spend on your relationship? Just think about it. I tell you, you spend much less on yourself! You spend much more money on your relationship than on yourself… and, of course, forget about service! We don't even spend 1% of what we have, on service to the public, for everybody's sake. Sharing and serving would enhance our ability to love, our ability to accept… and if you have that as a goal, and both move in this direction, together, I tell you, there will be no problem!

You know, I know one such couple. Do you know what the lady said to me, "*Panditji*, I'm with my husband for the past twenty-five years… and I *cannot* find one fault in him!"? She said, "I cannot find a single fault in this man!" Both of them are engaged in social service. It is so perfect! They meditate, they take time for themselves… This is what everyone aspires for, isn't it? So, when there's a common interest, a common goal, a common path, to move on, that nourishes the relationship, rather than focusing on the relationship all the time.

Love is essential in relationships, not mere attraction. In attraction, there's aggressiveness. In love, there is submission. This is the difference between love and attraction. Though attraction does form the first step, you cannot stand on the first step for too long. You have to move on to the next pedestal. That is love.

Service is an essential ingredient for a successful relationship… and if the relationship comes from the space of giving, rather than need, again, it is a good, "quality" relationship. Often we say, "Oh! I'm so bored; that's why I need a relationship!" I ask you, if you are bored with your own company, how much *more* boring are you for someone else?!

For a while, you look interesting, but in a few days, even weeks, though you won't express this to each other, you'll get bored with each other because there is no depth in you. Get rid of the boredom from within you… and be centred, really centred – understand your own Self, your own mind…and calm down. Don't be feverish. You know, you don't like to be with someone, who is feverish. The feverishness repels you, unless you're so full of compassion that nobody's feverishness matters anymore! But especially in relationships, feverishness reduces the charm.

When you are in love with someone, you just go on talking, talking… and talking! There's no need to pull so many words out of those mouths! You can just sit quietly with a smile, watch the sunset, or be with them. Learn to be with the person, whom you love, *in silence*. This is an art by itself.

When you are in such deep love, you don't know, what you are talking! Then you go on saying things that you regret afterwards. Sometimes, you don't know that what you have said may hurt the other person. The intellect is not sharp, not fully alert, when you are in love. You're in a daze… and in that daze, you don't know what you are blabbering, or what your blabbering will do to the other person – what effect it will bring on the other person. But later on, after ten days, or maybe ten years, you'll find out that whatever you said in a light way has affected the other person very deeply… How many of you have experienced this? Isn't this true almost everywhere?

When you're centred, and when you let go of your feverishness, then you're not bored with yourself – then your charm becomes long-lasting. The nearer a person comes to you, the more the charm will be there. That is the secret of being centred, of being connected with the Self, deep within us.

You know, Ananda once asked Buddha, "Buddha, for forty years, I've been watching you, day and night… and everyday, you're more charming! What is it? I can't get over it! Every moment I see you, you're still new!"

That is the nature of our consciousness. The mind is not a stagnant lake. It is a flowing river – a fast flowing river. You see, what I'm saying? When we float with the river, we are in the moment… Live every moment like that! Don't just brood over the past, or be anxious about the future.

One of the characteristics of love is eternity. When you are in love with somebody, you want that moment to be eternal: "We should be like this forever and ever!" You want it to be like that forever, for always! You use these words, don't you? "Always!"

Love is immortal – meaning, beyond time… and that is what we aim at… and *that* is our nature, our source. Just take some time off… and go within your silence. Then you will see, so much strength comes out of you, and from that, your charm becomes eternal, your love becomes unconditional.

You have heard of unconditional love so many times, but just words won't help. This has to come from our presence. You see what I'm saying? You can lecture on love for hours together, but if it is not radiating in your presence, nobody can make it out. This is something, we do not attend to – our presence. Our presence gets drained. Initially, when there was presence, there was attraction – but the moment, the presence dilutes, attraction dies out. You simply hang around. You are bored, but you still don't want to say that you are bored, and hurt the other person. The other person is also thinking in the same way! So inside the mind, there is a big gap, though outside, in your expression, you don't express it. How does one bridge this?

This is only possible by improving our presence. See, when you get off a plane, the hostesses greet you by saying, "Have a nice day!" They don't really mean it!

But, when the same words come from someone very close and dear to you – like your grandmother, your mother, your sister, your brother – they touch your heart. This is because those words carry a flood of feeling behind them. So, when you have to say to someone, "I love you," even if it's just once, those words should carry a flood of feeling, instead of repeating the phrase oh, so many times!

You feel so bitter, and yet you call and say, "Hello, honey!" You're saying, "honey" on the outside, but inside, you feel bitter about that! Perhaps to cover the bitterness, you keep saying, "Honey, honey, honey…!" These words do not carry the feeling… and that's why relationships become such a big mess, and break so often.

Our love doesn't grow old. Our love doesn't become ancient. Our love dies infant deaths. Love relationships have the highest mortality rate in our society today. Isn't it? Hmmm?

Take time for your self – a week in a year… and be with nature. Just observe the waves in the ocean, the birds… Don't talk! All that talk doesn't give us anything! It doesn't convey so much – it only creates more and more confusion. Isn't it? Of course, words are essential, but they have a limit. The purpose of words is to create silence within you. The purpose of words is to create peace within you. If your words create peace, then you have used them right. If they stir you, and create growth in you, then you've used them right. But often, when we're in a daze, we use words, which have no meaning, no depth and no sense. Look into the eyes of a child… They radiate so much love. Their presence is full of love.

We have to cleanse our presence. We never do anything to cleanse our mind, or our presence. Isn't it? See, you feel angry, agitated, tense, jealous, upset... These give rise to words that get transformed into particles in the body... and they remain in some form – either in a structured or chemical form – in our body. Only through deep rest, proper breathing, or fasting, can you eliminate them. If you meditate, take some time off – even half an hour a week, just once a week – and breathe through them, you can eliminate them and make your presence come up, come alive.

Suppose you don't believe in breathing, never mind! Then you fast, but again, don't fast on your own, or by reading books. Fast under some good guidance – under a doctor, or someone, who knows about fasting. Under their guidance, fast for ten, twelve or fifteen days, on water and juice. Then also, toxins from your body, get released. Fasting does help, but it needs much more work because when you come out of fasting, you have to come out slowly. If you don't have time to breathe, where is the time for you to fast?!

Meditation! Meditation is nothing to be afraid of! Meditation is for deep rest, total relaxation, a wakeful rest. Your eyes are closed, but you're awake inside… and you are letting your body relax very deeply. You can eliminate toxins through meditation also, and when the toxins are eliminated, your presence becomes palatable, beautiful and lovely. The charm in you will grow more and more!

You might have gone to beauticians, had make-up done, and got yourself dressed and everything, but if you are uptight inside, it shows on your face, doesn't it? You may not be very beautiful, but if you have the charm of your mind, the innocence of your consciousness, then that is something beyond words. We are endowed with this quality at birth, but somewhere on the way, we have lost it.

Just walk into a kindergarten class, and look into the faces of the children… See what joy, what peace, what beauty, there is. Then go to the higher classes… and the college rooms – and you see the vast difference.

Is this, what we are doing? Is this, what education is? We are spending our time, money and energy on becoming more and more unhappy and stressed – losing all that we are born with. Isn't it? See your children – are they growing happier, day-by-day, or more miserable, day-by-day? Tell me, what is the situation? Is this, what you want for your children – to make them more miserable, day-by-day – all because we have not taught them, how to cleanse their minds, how to elevate their being, or how to get rid of negative emotions, when these come into their lives. These things play an important role.

So, understanding the other person, giving them space, maintaining your centred-ness, and letting go of feverishness, are all essential to a successful relationship. A relationship needs a lot more attention and effort because it's not dragging someone along – it's like two wheels moving *together*. I don't have to say this. You all know about it. So, right perception, right observation and right expression… and as I said, in the beginning, I'm not an authority on this subject! So, if you have other opinions, other questions, or other ideas, I would like to listen to you!

❄❄❄

YOUR QUESTIONS ANSWERED...

Q: *Does having a family and children keep someone from enlightenment?*

Not at all! It is only your hankering for enlightenment that can keep you away from it! In fact, enlightenment brings you to a big family and more children!

Q: *Why does it feel like some people are more special to us than others?*

It is because of your likes and dislikes... and these can also change, can't they? Ask this question to your self. Wonder, why you appreciate some qualities in these people – are they qualities, which you think, you do not have?

Q: *Our strongest negative feelings are directed towards those, we love the most. How can we avoid this, while maintaining the affection?*

By developing awareness, and spending a little time in knowledge, in meditation – and by doing this very often, not just once in a while! Spend your thoughts on the knowledge about the impermanence of everything and the permanence in spirit. Then, a lot of difference comes up naturally in life.

Q: *How does one cope up with the death of someone close to you*?

You know, when someone very close to you, dies, there is a vacuum. This person was walking, talking, doing all these things, and suddenly, he (or she) is not there. A vacuum is created… and time will heal it. Your understanding of the world, of life, your broadened awareness, time, or meditation – all these things – will help you cope up with the situation.

Q: *How can I not always blame myself for something that goes wrong with a close acquaintance?*

You know, you should leave this "always"! I want to be happy "always"... "Always" this... Why *always*? Take life as it comes! Sometime you are upset. It is okay to be upset. Sometimes you are angry. It is okay to be angry. Life does not stop for anything. It moves. Just move with the flow.

Q: *Some therapists say that a relationship between a husband and wife is improved, if they can be in touch* *with their feelings, and share these with each other. Is this true? Should they share some feelings or all of them?*

Your feelings change... They change so often! But, when you express your feelings, the other person takes them in "deeper", maintaining the impressions, and holding on to them. They may feel, you feel like that, all the time. It is all right to share – we must share, but again, you have to use your discretion. You have to understand your own feelings first. You don't need to share everything. It may only create more confusion and a gap.

Q: *Why do people get angry and hurt their loved ones? How can we stop doing this?*

Hurt is part of love. It is *because* you have loved, that you feel hurt. Nobody *tries* to hurt you. When you are in love, you are in such a delicate space, that a simple action – even an act of non-deliberate ignoring – hurts you; an act of indifference hurts you. It's not that "they" are being indifferent deliberately; they are indifferent due to circumstances or situations, but, because you are in love, you are in such a vulnerable, delicate situation, condition and state of mind – That is why these things hurt you very quickly. Take "hurt" as *part* of love… and then you will feel very safe.

It is because you love, that in such deep love, small things hurt – If your loved one does not smile at you, it hurts you – otherwise, it is not a big deal.

Don't see intentions behind other people's mistakes. Suppose, you love somebody, and that person has hurt you, don't see that he (or she) has hurt you *intentionally*. Don't see that! When *you* make a mistake, what do you do, or say, very often?

You say, "It just happened! I didn't mean it!"

However, when *someone else* makes a mistake, you say, "Oh! That person did this *intentionally!*" Don't you do this?

Now tell me, haven't *your* actions hurt *somebody* at *sometime*, or the other? You have also hurt someone, at sometime, through your actions, your words, your behaviour…

Anger, hurt… are all a part of love. You have to take them "in that way". It is because you love somebody, that you get angry... and it is because they love you, that they get angry with you – otherwise, they would be indifferent to you. Anger indicates love behind it. Do you see what I am saying? If someone is angry, you should be happy because that means they love you!

Q: *If a person thinks he (or she) is very generous and honest, but lacks patience and self-tolerance, then how does he (or she) cope in life with a suitable partner?*

Now listen! Life is very complex. There is no direct simple mathematics! You will have to deal with life in a very complex manner. There is no set formula that says we have to deal with things like this or like that. When you think that you are very honest, you are being righteous… and without your knowledge, you become a little stiff inside: "I am righteous. So the others are wrong." You point your fingers at others… and you become intolerant.

When you recognize there are flaws in you, you become supple. You are able to accommodate the flaws in other people. That's why it is said: "Do a good deed… and forget it".

It's not only your vices, or bad qualities, that will harm you – even good qualities can make you so stiff, so rude, and so angry! So both, good and bad qualities, harm you. That is why it is said – surrender them both. Relax… and let go!

There are three types of perfection – perfection in action, perfection in speech and perfection in feelings. Many, who have perfection in their actions and speech, do not have that at their feelings-level. Some have perfection in their feelings and speak very well, but their actions will not be perfect. Perfection in feeling, perfection in speech, and perfection in action, is called *trikarana shuddhi* – to be perfect in all the three apparatuses.

Q: *My relationships with people are changing. Before, when I was in any relationship, I had this tendency to want to hold on to it, or to be possessive. Now I find that I'm more like – If a person is there, he (or she) is there, and if he (or she) is not there, it's fine. Whatever they choose to do is okay. I have been able to come to that space of accepting, and allowing them to just be, while still being in that unconditional state of love. Is this okay?*

That's beautiful, isn't it? It brings freedom to both!

See, what is really bothering you, is doubt, isn't it? Doubts bother us, if they are not in the "right place". Doubts arise – this is part of life! They only need to be put in the proper place. Notice that your doubts are about something that is positive – that, which is good. You never doubt that, which is negative! Have you thought about it?

When you are depressed, you never doubt if you are *really* depressed! If you are unhappy, you never ask yourself, "Am I *really* unhappy?" If you are angry, you never doubt your anger!

But, if someone says, "I love you!" – you doubt that, wondering, "What is he (or she) up to?? Is this person really in love with me, or is he (or she) just saying so? You doubt love. You doubt compassion. When you are happy, you doubt your happiness. You ask, "Is this what I want? I am not sure if this is what I really wanted? I am not sure…" – A doubt "comes". But, you don't doubt something that you don't want. Have you observed this simple factor, this simple thing?

We doubt the goodness in people, but we take all the negative aspects in life for granted; we take them to be the truth, reality – whether they are in us, or in other people. Place the doubt in negativity – whether it is in you, in someone else, or in the world.

We take it for granted that everybody in the world is hopeless, that everything is negative, that it's all horrible. Then, we try to find trust in this person, or that person… and it becomes difficult for us.

Take another standpoint: "Basically, everybody *is* good!" Even if somebody is a criminal, inside him, deep inside him, he *is* good. Due to his stress, circumstances, or situation, he is doing something, which he himself, does not realise, or know… So, if you go to one's depths, you will see that basically, everyone is good, everyone is lovable… and from this standpoint, you will see that trust in goodness grows, and that you doubt anger and other negative emotions. Life will be very rewarding this way – don't you think?

Q: *Is it okay for a woman to love another woman?*

If you are saying it is "love", then its meaning is different. It is okay to love *everybody*! It is *essential* for a human being to love everybody and everything in this world.

If what you mean by "love" is "physical attraction", then, I would not say it is either good, or bad – or that you should, or shouldn't. Before taking any further steps, observe and look into your self. Observe the feelings, emotions, and sensations in the body… That will free you from all the fear, guilt, or any other unpleasant things that you store within you.

Q: *The new Pontificate (Vatican) is expected to take a rigid stance on issues like those of gay relationships. What do the ancient scriptures say about these matters?*

As far as the ancient scriptures are concerned, there is neither mention, nor prohibition of it. One thing the ancient scriptures say, as far as I know, is that every human being is made up of *both* Mother and Father – half-female, half-male. The male tendency may be dominant; sometimes the female tendency may be dominant. It is a biological phenomenon. So if people are bound to have such tendencies, they should just acknowledge it.

Q: *Are you approving of gay marriages? Would you conduct gay marriages?*

Conducting marriages is not part of spirituality at all. It is a religious thing. Spirituality simply makes you aware that you are *spirit* and it uplifts you from all tendencies, whether you are for, or against, or paranoid about the sexuality of other people. All this is not concerned with spirituality. Spirituality makes you realize that you are *not just flesh*. You are light. So there is gender equality in spirituality! Religion will not give you gender equality, whereas in spirituality, whether you are a mother, or a father, it doesn't matter – you are equal.

Q: *But here, we are not talking about parenthood...?*

I am talking about the male and female tendencies in a person. Depending on whatever tendencies are strongest in the system, biologically, this will accordingly reflect in one's life and sexuality. So I think, one should see that one is not just flesh because it's a temporary thing. Tendencies are temporary, but the spirit is *much more* than tendencies. You are the spirit, which is all light, all love, wisdom and knowledge. Your identification must shift from gender to spirit… and this is exactly what spirituality means – to rise above the tendencies that are impermanent.

We have seen that many straight people "get" gay tendencies, sometimes... and this creates fear in them. They are so scared about what is happening to them. When they start meditating, they rise above this, and become natural and loving. Even people, who brand themselves as being gay, suddenly find themselves being attracted to the opposite sex… and it creates big confusion. This is why I say that you should not label yourself. You are much more than your tendencies. You *are* the beautiful spirit, and if that is also a label, it is better to have this label, than any other.

Q: *I'm personally heterosexual, but here in Europe, and I believe in America as well, there are many, who practice homosexuality or bisexuality. I have many friends, who do. Can this influence the unfolding of the human being, or spiritual growth, in one way or the other?*

It is not the outside figure or object, but rather the sensation or pleasure that you feel inside, that is important. The "outside" is just a mirror that brings out the pleasure that you are on the inside. Do you see what I'm saying?

It is the movement of *prana*, of energy – because none of the tendencies, tastes, likes, or dislikes in a person, are permanent. They keep changing. Like I said before, I've seen many heterosexuals suddenly get the urge for the same sex. This shakes them. They say, "What is wrong with *me*?! I was alright all these years…" Also, many people, who think of themselves as homosexuals, suddenly feel attracted to people of the opposite sex and they also experience the same problem. So, what I would say is, you don't have to label yourself as something, or somebody.

Again, I say, instead of giving so much importance to a piece of flesh – to the outside – turn within… and look at the spirit. *That* is the source of joy.

You know, the joy of sex is only for one minute, but the joy of the Being is one thousand times more than that! So it's this sustained joy, a sustained flow of energy, within you, that makes you realize, you are not just a body, you are not a man, or a woman, you are not a piece of flesh… You are light. You are spirit. When we "get into" this identification, we see that there is so much joy in life – unshakeable and lasting joy!

Of course, sex is a part of life – we are not denying this. What I'm saying is, as you experience sex, and go through this in life, you can turn more towards the spirit. Then we support the evolution of life in that direction. It's a very good balance – not denying, while at the same time, not indulging – and by just attending to the *prana*, to the breath, this happens automatically.

Q: *If we're all one, does it matter, which partner I choose for my life? Please tell me something about love and what I need to do for a long partnership.*

You know, a partnership is something you don't put your head into and decide upon! It's your heart, which draws you towards it. But at the same time, you cannot simply be swayed away by it – you also need to use a little bit of your intellect. So you need a certain balance. If you just get into it, only on an impulse, you'll be in trouble… and you'll put others in trouble too! If you just look at someone and think, "Oh! This is such a nice partner for me!" – and the next day, your heart goes elsewhere… and on the third day, your heart goes somewhere else – This won't work!

At the same time, if you keep thinking with your head, it won't work either: "Who should be my partner? Who is my partner?"

So to choose your partner, you need a little intellect (10%), you need 70% - 90% heart… and 20% luck!!

It's a gamble! A couple divorced each other after 45 years of marriage! They were both in their 70s. In court, they said, "We *never* got along with each other all these years. For not a single day, did we get along!" Forty years of marriage and that's what they said! They never got along, but then, *how* did these forty odd years pass?! What was it all about? The whole problem, in court, was over a *chair*!! This isn't a joke – It's reality! This happened in California. An old man took his wife to court for not letting him keep his chair! He was so attached to that chair! They were 70 and 75 (or 74) years old respectively – they were that old… and they both said that they never got along, all forty years of their married life together. Can you believe that?!

When something goes wrong, you suddenly feel, you *never* got along *at all*! It is true! We always externalize and generalize our problems! Have you noticed that? Suppose, you meet ten people, who are sick, what do you say? You say, "*Everyone* here, in Germany, is falling sick!"

It is true you didn't get along, but you come up with very fantastic ideas and externalize the problem.

You say, "I always make mistakes!" Do you *always* make mistakes? Really? No! You make a mistake *sometimes*, but when that one mistake "appears", you say, "I always make mistakes…" – as if you have always been making mistakes. You blame yourself. You blame, and feel sorry for yourself. Do you get what I'm saying? We have to get out of this cycle, through our own determination, through our own will.

In a partnership, if both partners come from a space of "I want to contribute," then it's a healthy partnership. But, if both partners think, "What will I get out of the partnership?" – then, it will not remain a healthy partnership. Love is in *giving*, not taking. Love *means* giving. "How much have I given? What can I give? How can I contribute?" – That is love. In love, whatever you give, you still feel you have not given enough – you feel, what you have given, is little. If you feel you have given enough, that means, there is some dilution in that love… Hmm? However, if it *is* that way, that is how it is – you can't "make" a mood. If you feel there is no love, then you can't force yourself: "Oh, I must love, I *must* love!" No! It's not possible! That's how it is. You have to accept it. Do you see what I'm saying? No wife can force herself to love her husband. No husband can force himself to love his wife. That's why, don't go seeking love. Just relax! Only, when you're free from tension, free from confusion, can you ever experience love. Love is a happening! Love is a gift to you. It's not something you can cultivate. You can't say, "Okay! I'm going to do this exercise… and then I'm going to love!" Not possible!

Usually, the problem between men and women is that the wife (the woman), wants assurance from the man that she's loved, and the husband (the man), loves, but he does not know how to *prove* to his wife that he loves her! This is the problem in the world. A man is not expressive, like a woman is, but a woman demands an expression of love, which a man is unable to give. He cannot tell her in words – atleast not as much as the woman expects. This is the problem. Trying to prove your love for someone is the most difficult thing to do.

You can love somebody, but if they ask for proof, it becomes a headache! Someone asks, you, "Prove to me that you *really* love me!" You think, "My goodness!" You can do that for one, two, three, four days… and afterwards, what can you do?!

That man doesn't want to come home now at all! He

thinks, "Oh! My God! When I go home, my wife will demand: 'Come on! Prove to me that you really love me!' Oh! My God! I've got a headache! What will I do now?!" So he gives his wife all kinds of excuses: "I have work, I have this, I have that…"

It is the same with men and women. It's the same thing. A husband also cannot ask the lady in the house to prove her love all the time: "Does she really love me or not?"

We have to remember two things – a man's ego, and a woman's emotions, should not be hurt.

A wife should always uplift her man's ego. The day a wife tells her man, "You are a vegetable! You are good for nothing!" – even if he only has a little talent, he will lose that also, because a man cannot stand without the ego. If you hurt a man's ego, you cut his very basis.

Similarly, if you tell a woman, "Your brother is no good! Your parents are no good!" If you tell her anything, related to her parents, or relatives – that is out! She is off! You cannot hurt a woman's emotions. She is emotional. That emotional support needs to be given. She needs to be comforted. You have to express your emotions to her, otherwise, she feels lonely and unwanted. If you don't appreciate her, she gets so upset. If you don't say, "Oh! You are wearing a nice dress today!" or "You cooked nicely!" – she feels that nobody cares for her. If her husband comes to eat food, and it's just business: "*Haan*... Okay! Who came? What are..." – she gets upset. If a man doesn't take the time to cater to a woman's emotions, he cannot do justice to her.

Similarly, a woman should always uplift the ego of her husband – *that's all* he's looking for! The whole world can tell him, "You are useless," but, if his wife tells him, "You are useless!" – he *cannot* take it! The world can tell him that he is hopeless, but his wife has to tell him, "No! You are best!"

❄❄❄

The Art of Living
&
The International Association for Human Values

Transforming Lives...

The Founder

Gurudev Sri Sri Ravi Shankar

Gurudev Sri Sri Ravi Shankar is a universally revered spiritual and humanitarian leader. His vision of a violence-free, stress-free society through the reawakening of human values has inspired millions to broaden their spheres of responsibility and work towards the betterment of the world. Born in 1956 in southern India, Gurudev was often found deep in meditation as a child. At the age of four, he astonished his teachers by reciting the Bhagwad Gita, an ancient Sanskrit scripture. He has always had the unique gift of presenting the deepest truths in the simplest of words.

Gurudev established The Art of Living, an educational and humanitarian Non-Governmental Organisation that works in special consultative status with the Economic and Social Council (ECOSOC) of the United Nations in 1981. Present in over 156 countries, it formulates and implements lasting solutions to conflicts and issues faced by individuals, communities and nations. In 1997, he founded the International Association for Human Values (IAHV) to foster human values and lead sustainable development projects. Gurudev has reached out to more than 300 million people worldwide through personal interactions, public events, teachings, The Art of Living workshops and humanitarian initiatives. He has brought to the masses ancient practices which were traditionally kept exclusive, and has designed many self development techniques which can easily be integrated into daily life to calm the mind and instill confidence and enthusiasm. One of Gurudev's most unique offerings to the world is the Sudarshan Kriya, a powerful breathing technique that facilitates physical, mental, emotional and social well-being.

Numerous awards have been bestowed upon Gurudev Sri Sri Ravi Shankar which includes Padma Vibhushan (India's second highest civilian award) and the highest civilian awards from Paraguay, Mongolia and Colombia. Gurudev has addressed several international forums, including the United Nations Millennium World Peace Summit (2000), World Economic Forum (2001, 2003), World Summit On Ethics In Sports at FIFA Headquarters, Zurich (2014, 2016), UNESCO (2015), Parliaments of France, Britain, Norway (2016) and others.

Gurudev has played a key role in conflict resolution across the world including Colombia, Kashmir, Iraq, Ivory Coast, Naxal inhabited regions of India, and many other places.

Follow Sri Sri on:

Twitter - @srisri

Facebook - www.facebook.com/SriSriRaviShankar

Website - www.srisri.org

YouTube - www.youtube.com/srisri

Instagram - www.instagram.com/srisriravishankar

LinkedIn - www.linkedin.com/in/srisriravishankar

The Art of Living

In Service Around The World

Founded in 1981 by Gurudev Sri Sri Ravi Shankar, The Art of Living is engaged in stress-elimination programs and service initiatives. The organization operates globally in 156 countries with one of the largest volunteer bases in the world and has touched the lives of over 370 million people.

The organisation works in special consultative status with the Economic and Social Council (ECOSOC) of the United Nations, participating in a variety of committees and activities related to health and conflict resolution.

In 1997, Gurudev Sri Sri Ravi Shankar also founded the International Association for Human Values (IAHV) to coordinate sustainable development projects, nurture human values and coordinate conflict resolution in association with The Art of Living. In India, Africa and South America, the two sister organizations' volunteers are spearheading sustainable growth in rural communities, and have already reached out to 40,212 villages.

The Art of Living movement has spread peace and transformation across communities through diverse humanitarian projects.

- Conflict Resolution
- Alleviating pain in War Zones
- Relieving trauma in Post Terror Attacks
- Disaster Relief
- Environment
- Education
- Empowerment of Women
- Prisoner Rehabilitation
- Rural Transformation

The Art of Living Programs

The Art of Living programs are guided by Gurudev Sri Sri Ravi Shankar's philosophy of peace: "Unless we have a stress-free mind and a violence-free society, we cannot achieve world peace." To help individuals get rid of stress and experience inner peace, The Art of Living offers stress-elimination programs which include breathing techniques, meditation and yoga. They cater to every age group - children, youth, adults and every section of society – rural communities, governments, corporate houses, etc. These programs have helped millions around the world to overcome stress, depression and violent tendencies. Emphasizing holistic living and personal self-development, the programs facilitate the complete blossoming of an individual's full potential. The cornerstone of all our workshops is the Sudarshan Kriya, a unique and potent breathing practice.

Introductory Programs:

- **The Happiness Program (Age 18+):**
  The 3-day program equips participants with practical knowledge and techniques to unlock their deepest potential and bring fullness to life.
- **Sahaj Samadhi Meditation (Age 18+):**
  Meditation technique that deeply relaxes the mind and rejuvenates the system.

- **ART Excel (Age 8-13):**
  Introduce your children to spirituality, nurture human values, inculcate self-discipline, and develop their personality to be healthy and well-rounded.
- **YES (Age 14-18):**
  Dynamic and innovative educational program for both high school and college students.
- **Prajñā Yoga (Age 5-18):**
  Helps children tap into the inherent intuitive abilities of the mind.

For more information please visit: www.artofliving.org

International Centres

INDIA
21st km, Kanakapura Road, Udayapura,
Bangalore - 560 082, Karnataka
Telephone: 0091 - 80-67262626 / 27 / 28
Email: info@srisripublications.com

GERMANY
Bad Antogast 1, 77728 Oppenau, Baden-Württemberg
Telephone: 0049 - 7804-973-90
Email: info@artofliving.de

CANADA
13 Infinity Road, St. Mathieu du Parc, Quebec G0X 1N0
Telephone: 001 - 819-532-3328
Email: artdevivre@artofliving.org

USA
639 Whispering Hills Rd, Boone, NC 28607
Telephone: 001 - 828-263-4910
Email: info@artoflivingretreatcenter.org

www.srisriravishankar.org
www.artofliving.org
www.iahv.org